My experiences with Saturn in the fifth house In astrology

A. My experiences

B. Look inside and work hard and do my best

A. My experiences

I did not have a lot of fun in my life, or at least felt that way (

maybe because it's Saturn but I got to have fun at least sometimes and work hard at something . Saturn does not reward someone who does not work hard on something or themselves, My answer, work hard but I do the best I can.

Saturn ,lord of karma

SATURN<THE TASKMASTER FATHER TIME in the fifth house deals with lessons on

matters of romantic love, artistic expression and children as well as heart issues

like love !!!!
and acceptance
Restrict love!!!until later

Saturn rules the bones, it rules time. Saturnian themes take time for it to develop. For me in Saturn in the fifth house. I had to learn fifth house lesssons like love ,because I was deprived of it, pretty much early in my life. Saturn in the fifth house astrologically can delay or prevent love or romantic relationships from happening depending on aspects in general. For me < the general astrological 5th house stuff was true . I was restricted or did not find the right romantic lover early in my life; but I did learn that love is really on the inside.

Saturn does point to self love as an answer because it is

not really a bad planet, It is my best friend because if I work hard on myself, my expression then I can be rewarded but on my merits not by chance. I strongly look to

Jupiter because Jupiter is the answer to keeping positive and seeing luck .

Jupit

Jupiter

Jupiter (luck)

B. Look inside and work hard and do the best I can

My Jupiter aspects can soften Saturn 's hardships, the coldness that

Saturn has can make this house placement painful as it has for me but love in the reality sense, love for who I am and with others who like me for me and not for what I have. In other words . I cannot hate myself or love a bad person, a criminal lover, someone who will use me — that is not love. It cannot be something in an illusion but someone who really likes me and respects me and my boundaries, More importantly within , that my take on Saturn in the fifth house of astrology.

I do not know
what is going
to happen in
the future but
my take with
Saturn in the

fifth house. Love myself , work hard on my self, expression and do the best I can because that is all I can do . DO THE BEST I CAN And let god take care the rest .

DO THE BEST I CAN

DO THE BEST I CAN . LOVE THYSELF <BE

HONEST AS BESt AS I CAN

www.ingramcontent.com/pod-product-compliance
Lightning Source LLC
LaVergne TN
LVHW011431080426
835512LV00005B/385